Fidget Wisely

10 WAYS TO TEACH
MINDFULNESS SKILLS TO
KIDS WHO CAN'T SIT STILL

A book for parents, teachers, and therapists

By: Kirsten May Keach MA, MFT

TABLE OF CONTENTS

INTRODUCTION

In this book, Fidget Wisely: 10 ways to teach mindfulness skills to kids who can't sit still, you will learn practical, hands-on strategies for bringing mindfulness into the everyday life of your children. This book is designed for busy parents, teachers, and therapists who are looking for new ways to approach children. This book provides detailed instructions on how to make mindfulness a part of your children's daily routine. All of the activities offered in this book are things that I utilize myself in my practice as a Psychotherapist and as a Yoga Teacher.

HOW IT ALL BEGAN

For my first job after graduate school, I had the privilege of working as a therapist in an elementary school. I very quickly had a full caseload of kids. Children were coming to my office frustrated and anxious. The teachers that sent them were equally frustrated. The conversations with teachers and administrators went something like this: "He/she is a smart kid with a lot of potential but…he just doesn't listen" or "She won't sit still" or "Her behavior is disrupting the other students," and so on. The conversations with parents began in a similar way, "He is a really sweet kid… he just doesn't listen" or "He refuses to do his homework" or "He fights when it's time to get ready for school in the morning." The list went on. I call this the "He/she is a great kid, but… story."

This story began to permeate my days. There was something standing between these kids and being successful. It was my job to identify and dissolve the "but" standing in the way of these kids and their success. What I found was that for the most part, these kids had poor emotional regulation skills. This means that they had difficulty managing their feelings and emotions. This made it difficult for them to thrive in a classroom setting.

I began to teach kids emotional regulation skills through mindfulness and yoga activities. I integrated the skills I learned as a yoga teacher and things I learned living in a Thai Buddhist Monastery into my work as a therapist. I made all of these skills kid-friendly. Some of the things in this book are my original ideas, and some of them are things that I've learned from other people and adapted.

The kids loved learning mindfulness skills. To my surprise, they caught on like wildfire, and teachers and students started requesting more. Since this initial experience, I have gone on to teach mindfulness skills to kids in a variety of school and therapeutic settings. At the time when this book was written, these skills were being taught to 200 students as a part of a 7-week program. The activities presented in this book will not solve all of the problems that participating children have. Nor are they guaranteed to produce children with excellent self-regulation skills. What these activities do is provide parents, teachers, and therapists with another option. They offer something else to try when nothing else is working. Having another option can help to provide space. And sometimes, space is enough to create a change.

WHAT IS "MINDFULNESS" AND WHY DOES IT MATTER?

Mindfulness is simultaneously a skill and a state of being. John Kabat-Zinn (2003, p. 145) describes it as "the awareness that emerges through paying attention on purpose, in the present moment, and non-judgmentally to the unfolding of experience." The UCLA Mindful Awareness Research Center defines mindful awareness as "paying attention to present moment experiences with openness, curiosity, and a willingness to be with what is." Mindful awareness based practices are exercises or activities that aim to increase and/or cultivate a state of mindfulness. Yoga and meditation are two popular forms of practice that cultivate mindful awareness.

Mindfulness based practice is gaining popularity as a method of treatment and prevention of physical and mental health issues ranging from depression and anxiety to obesity.

A New York Times article stated that mindfulness based practices are "now being offered by corporations like Google, Target and General Mills to their employees" (Hochman, 2013). Initial research into mindfulness based practices focused on the effectiveness of mindfulness on adults (Zoogman et al., 2014). This research is now being expanded to include mindfulness based programs for children. Research on the effectiveness of mindfulness-based practices with children is showing effectiveness with a wide range of issues. A meta-analysis of twenty research studies on mindfulness interventions with youth determined that mindfulness interventions were helpful and produced superior results in control groups (Zoogman et al., 2014). Another study found that children who participated in mindfulness based education groups had an increase in optimism, socially competent behaviors, and self-concept (Schonert-Reichl & Lawlor, 2010).

MINDFUL AWARENESS PRACTICES IN SCHOOLS

Mindful awareness practices are being developed, implemented, and researched to be utilized within schools. Mindfulness based interventions are being added to school curriculums across the United States including schools in California, Pennsylvania, New York, and Oregon (Brown, 2007). These interventions are being brought into schools at a time when American schools are facing a crisis. Children and school personnel are not equipped to deal with the stress they are facing.

MINDFULNESS FOR THIS BOOK

For the purpose of this book, I will be using Jon Kabit-Zin's definition of mindfulness as "paying attention on purpose to the present moment" (2003, p. 145). This book presents a series of activities that you can utilize to help children bring their awareness to the present moment. I have personally found all of these activities to be helpful in my work with children. I encourage you to try them, and experience for yourself what works and what does not work for your child.

TIPS FOR USING THIS BOOK

Three rules of teaching mindfulness to kids

1. Have fun

2. Keep it simple- all of the activities in this book are designed to be simple.

3. Do what feels comfortable. If at any time you or your child feel uncomfortable, just stop.

How to get the most out of mindfulness

All of the activities in this book take practice in order for children to get the most benefit. I recommend the following strategies in order to help implement these approaches on a regular basis.

Create a mindfulness routine

Carving out a time each day where you and your child, or group of children, practice mindfulness is a great way to strengthen the practice. It is important that children learn and practice these activities when they are in a relatively calm state of mind.

This way when they become upset or agitated it is easier to utilize the practice because they already know how to use the techniques. It is difficult to teach a new skill to an upset child.

Developing a mindfulness safe space

Create a space in your home, office, or classroom where your child and/or children can go to access their mindfulness tools. This space is unique to you and can be as big as a room or as small as a shelf with a box of mindfulness supplies. What is important is that your child knows where it is and can access it when they need it.

MINDFULNESS STARTS WITH YOU

One of the best ways to teach children mindfulness is to develop your own mindfulness practice. This will help you to embody what you teach. This will help you to approach the activity from a place of mindful awareness. There are many ways that you can go about developing your own mindfulness practice.

Two Minutes of Silence

A few months ago, I walked into a room full of 6th graders. I had the privilege of being their substitute teacher for the day. The bell rang and it was time to begin class. I immediately began trying to wrangle kids. In a loud voice, I asked for their attention. I got no response. I saw a red hat go flying through the air. I heard a student make a hurtful comment towards another child. I watched as several kids pushed desks and chairs in a crude manner. I decided not to fight with these kids. I became very calm inside and stood at the front of the room in silence. I took a moment to be mindful myself. One by one, the kids noticed my presence.

They looked at me and sat down quietly in their chairs and became attentive. A few of the kid murmured things like "she is waiting." Within a few short minutes, I had the attention of the entire class. This all occurred without me having to yell, threaten, punish, or shame any of the students. Just the power of my silent aware presence pulled the attention of the room.

I chose to share this story because it exemplifies how my personal mindfulness practice impacted the way that I handled a difficult situation with a group of children. In this moment, I didn't use a fancy technique or teach the kids something new. I drew on my own practice, took a moment to become present and aware (aka mindful) and the rest unfolded.

I encourage all of you to research and explore mindfulness for yourself, and see what naturally unfolds from your own practice. Below is one very basic exercise you can use on yourself to begin exploring mindfulness. I recommend using this exercise before you start teaching mindfulness to children.

MINDFUL EXERCISE FOR PARENTS: TO DO BEFORE YOU START

This section provides instructions on how to use a breathing technique to become more present.

To Begin

Find a place where you can sit or stand comfortably. Straighten your spine so that you are sitting or standing tall. Take a big breath into your belly and then exhale all the air out.

The Exercise

> Imagine you are breathing into your feet.

> Take a big breath in through your nose, and imagine that your entire body is being filled with air, all the way down to the bottoms of your feet.

➤ Take a slow controlled exhalation through your nose allowing your exhalation to be longer than your inhalation.

➤ Continue this process three times.

➤ Once you complete your third round, release the breath.

➤ Take a moment to notice how your feel.

➤ Take a moment to look around the room or area you are in, and notice what is around you.

➤ Release the practice and continue with your day.

Conclusion

This breathing exercise can help you to calm down and relax. You can practice this activity throughout the day whenever you feel that you need it.

HOW TO MAKE A GLITTER JAR

Glitter Jar Supply List

- A 12 oz. mason jar (*or a plastic jar with a lid)
- 4 tablespoons of glitter glue
- 4+ tablespoons of fine glitter
- 1/2 cup of hot water
- 1 cup of cold water
- A stir stick

Rules For Making a Glitter Jar

- There is no such thing as too much glitter.
- Your jar is yours. Be as creative as you like.
- There is no such thing as a "perfect" glitter jar.
- Have fun!

13 Steps for Making a Glitter Jar

- STEP 1: Take the lid off your jar and place it to the side.
- STEP 2: Put 4 oz. of glitter glue into the jar (extra glue will not hurt your project)

STEP 3: Pour a 1/2 cup of hot water into the jar (adult supervision required)

STEP 4: Stir the glitter glue and hot water together until the glitter glue begins to break apart.

STEP 5: Add approximately 4 tablespoons of fine glitter. Add as many colors as you like.

STEP 6: Add cold water to the jar leaving two inches of space at the top of the jar.

STEP 7: Stir the contents of the jar until the glitter is evenly dispersed in the water.

STEP 8: Seal the lid on the jar. If the jar is cool, shake the jar allowing the contents to mix together. Decide if you are happy with your jar.

STEP 9: Add additional glitter if desired.

STEP 10: Fill the jar to the very top with water.

STEP 11: Glue around the inside of the lid with remaining glitter glue.

STEP 12: Screw the lid on tight.

STEP 13: Shake it up!

Creative Cat

Adding beads, sequins, or food coloring can make the jars more creative and dynamic.

How to use the glitter jar

Shake the glitter jar allowing the glitter to mix in with the water. Then, watch as the glitter slowly settles to the bottom. As you watch the glitter fall, you can do a variety of things such as noticing the different colors in the jar, counting the individual pieces of glitter, noticing how some pieces of glitter fall more slowly than other pieces. Allow yourself to notice what you notice.

DEEP BREATHING FOR KIDS

Introduction to Breathing Techniques

In this section of the book, we cover three breathing techniques that you can use with kids. We are always breathing. Therefore, breathing techniques are easily accessible. They are usable at any time and in any place.

The breathing activities in this book begin in a seated position. However, this is not necessary. Breathing activities can be performed standing up, lying down, or walking slowly. This is a great thing to use with kids who fidget frequently or have difficult staying in their seats.

SMELL THE BROWNIES

Smell the brownies

This chapter provides instructions on how to use a breathing technique that engages kids through using their sense of smell.

To Begin

Find a place where you can sit down comfortably. Once you are seated, stretch your spine up straight so that you are sitting nice and tall. If sitting does not work for you, stand up with a straight spine. You can put your back against a wall if it helps.

Take a big breath into your belly, and then exhale all the air out.

The Exercise

- Use your imagination to pretend that a huge tray of brownies, fresh from the oven, is sitting right in front of you.
- Now with your imagination, I want you to pick up one of those brownies and bring it up towards your face.
- Smell the brownie by taking a big breath in through your nose.

- The brownie is hot. Cool the brownie off by blowing through your mouth.
- We are going to do that again.
- Take a big breath in through your nose, smelling the brownie.
- Blow air out through your mouth, cooling the brownie.
- And one last time, smell the brownie, and cool it off.
- Take a big breath in through your nose, smelling the brownie.
- Blow air out through your mouth cooling the brownie off.
- Place your imaginary brownie back on the table in front of you.

Conclusion

This breathing exercise can help you to calm down and relax. You can practice this activity throughout the day whenever you feel that you need help to calm down and relax.

Creative Cat

This exercise can be performed using the imagination as is suggested above, or it can be done using props. For example, you can use a physical flower to this same activity. When using the flower, you would have the children smell the flower and then blow like the wind. Be creative in using images or props that you know your children love. This will help to keep them engaged.

LIZARD BREATH

Lizard Breath

This chapter provides instructions on how to use a breathing technique called Lizard Breath.

Teaching Tips

Kids enjoy this activity once they master the steps. It takes practice for them to get it down. This is especially true for younger kids. Before you begin the activity, introduce the kids to tongue rolling. Acknowledge that some people cannot roll their tongue. Approximately 75% of people are able to roll their tongue. The kids who cannot roll their tongue can complete the exercise by motioning the sides of their tongue towards the middle. This will create a crater like area in the middle of their tongue. This will work perfectly. Alternatively, kids who cannot roll their tongue can use a straw for the inhaling portion of the exercise.

Setup

Find a place where you can sit down comfortably. Once you are seated, stretch your spine up straight so that you are sitting nice and tall. If sitting does not work for you, stand up with a straight spine.

You can put your back against a wall if it helps. Take a big breath into your belly and then exhale all the air out.

The Exercise

- ➢ Stick out your tongue and roll it. If you are unable to roll your tongue, motion the sides of your tongue towards each other.

- ➢ Suck air in through your rolled tongue. You can make a slithering sound if you'd like.

- ➢ Once you are full of air, slither your tongue back into your mouth.

- ➢ Breath out through your nose.

- ➢ We are going to do that again.

- ➢ Stick out your tongue and roll it or attempt to roll it.

- ➢ Suck air in through your tongue with a slithering sound

- ➢ Slither your tongue back into your mouth.

- ➢ Breath out through your nose.

- ➢ Continue repeating the exercise until the kids seem to have completed at least one round successfully.

The Exercise

This breathing exercise can help you to calm down and relax. You can practice this activity throughout the day whenever you feel that you need help to calm down and relax.

The Exercise

This activity can be changed to "snake breath" or "reptile breath." To make this activity as fun as possible, add in a picture or video of a lizard, snake, or other reptile. Incorporate the reptile theme through the entire exercise. Help the kids visualize themselves as the reptile.

BUZZING BEE BREATH

Buzzing Bee Breath

This chapter provides instructions on how to use a breathing technique called Buzzing Bee Breath.

Teaching Tips

This breathing exercise often makes kids laugh because of the noise and the energy that is created. This exercise is genuinely joy creating. Watch the group and notice if the group is being silly or is having natural joy arise as a result of this process.

Setup

Find a place where you can sit down comfortably. Once you are seated, stretch your spine up straight so that you are sitting nice and tall. If sitting does not work for you, stand up with a straight spine. You can put your back against a wall if it helps. Take a big breath into your belly and then exhale all the air out. Notice how you feel right now.

THE EXERCISE

Learning how to Buzz

➤ Press your lips together tightly.

➤ Breath in through your nose.

➤ Push air through your lips while keeping them sealed.

➤ Allow this to create a buzzing sound like a bee.

Learning the hand position

➤ Place your pointer fingers above your eyebrows.

➤ Place your middle and ring fingers over your eyes. Be careful not to press too hard.

➤ Place your pinky fingers below your eyes.

➤ Place your thumbs over the small flap of skin just inside your ears.

Putting it together

➤ Place your pointer fingers above your eyebrows.

➤ Place your middle and ring fingers over your eyes. Be careful not to press too hard.

➤ Place your pinky fingers below your eyes.

- Place your thumbs over the small flap of skin just inside your ears.
- Press your lips together tightly.
- Breath in through your nose.
- Push air through your lips while keeping them sealed.
- Allow this to create a buzzing sound like a bee.
- Allow the sound to continue until it naturally comes to a stop
- Continue this process for several rounds.
- After completing the final round, release your hands and observe how you feel.

Putting it together

This breathing exercise can help you to calm down and relax. You can practice this activity throughout the day whenever you feel that you need help to calm down and relax. This breathing activity is also a great thing to do when you are feeling down and sad.

Putting it together

To make this activity as fun as possible, add in a picture or video of a bee. Playing the sound of a buzzing bee and then having the group mimic the sound of buzzing bees brings a dynamic element to this activity.

YOGA FOR KIDS

1. Focus on engagement not perfection.

2. Take turns leading and following.

3. Remember to have fun and keep things light.

4. Find ways to engage multiple senses – like having the kids make animal sounds or pretend they are the animal itself.

5. Place the children in a circle when teaching to a group.

CAT AND COW POSE

Cat and Cow Pose

This chapter provides instructions on how to teach a yoga pose called *Cat and Cow pose.*

Tips for Teachers

Kids get really engaged with this activity. Younger children can find it difficult to understand the difference between arching and bowing the spine. Demonstrate this pose before you teach it.

Set-up

To begin this exercise, all participants need to be on their hands and knees like a dog or cat.

THE EXERCISE

Cat Pose

➢ Begin by coming onto your hands and knees like a dog or cat.

➢ Place your hand underneath your shoulders and your knees underneath your hips.

- ➤ Straighten your spine.
- ➤ Imagine that you have a long tail extending from the base of your spine.
- ➤ Tuck your tail between your legs, and arch your back like a scared cat.
- ➤ Allow your head to drop towards that floor.

Cow Pose

- ➤ Point your tail towards the sky
- ➤ Create a bow shape with your spine like a cow
- ➤ Look up towards the sky.

Bring it Together

- ➤ Once you have the motions down for cat pose and cow pose bring them together.
- ➤ Move into cat pose on your out breath and cow pose on you out breath.

Creative Cat

For an engaging addition to this pose, instruct the kids to make cat (meow) and cow (moo) sounds when they are in the pose. This is especially fun for younger kids.

FROG POSE

Frog Pose

This chapter provides instructions on how to teach a yoga pose called *Frog Pose*.

Tips for Teachers

The instructions written here begin from a standing position. However, it is easy to get into this pose from a seated position like crisscross applesauce. This can be a great pose to use when your group is seated in a circle on the floor.

Setup

Find a place where you can stand comfortably. Begin this process by coming into mountain pose. Stand with both feet together or hip width distance apart. Stand with a straight spin. Bring your shoulders up towards your ears and then roll them down your back. This is mountain pose.

The Exercise

> Spread your feet 1 foot apart.
> Turn your right foot towards the right and your left foot.

- Squat down towards the floor allowing your knees to open to each side.

- Place your hands together at the center of your chest.

- Place your elbows inside your knees, keeping your palms at the center of your chest.

- Stick out your tongue and make a ribbit sound.

- Complete the pose by taking a big deep breath into your body and then exhaling.

- Place your hands on the floor and stand up into a forward fold.

- Slowly roll up to a standing position.

Creative Cat

To make this activity as fun as possible, add in a picture or video of a frog. Playing sounds of singing frogs or nature sounds brings a dynamic element to this activity.

LION POSE

This chapter provides instructions on how to teach a yoga pose called *Lion Pose*.

Tips for Teachers

This exercise is both a yoga pose and a breathing exercise in one. The breathing portion of this pose needs to be demonstrated before you teach it. If kids are uncomfortable on their knees, they can remain seated in a crisscross applesauce position or sit in a chair and follow the rest of the instruction.

Set-up

Begin this pose seated on your knees.

THE EXERCISE

Lion Position

- ➤ Begin by sitting on your knees.
- ➤ Place your hands on your knees.
- ➤ Stretch your spine up tall.

Lion Position

> ➤ Remain seated in the Lion Position.

> ➤ Take a deep breath in through your nose.

> ➤ Lean forward with your torso.

> ➤ Stick your tongue out as far as you can. Make a roar like a lion as you exhale.

Creative Cat

Adding the roar sound from a real lion adds depth and playfulness to this activity.

HOW TO MAKE A RICE BOX

Rice Box Supply List

- ➢ A plastic tote box with a lid
- ➢ 10-20 lbs. of rice
- ➢ 2+ funnels
- ➢ 2+ plastic cups

Rice Box Rules

- ➢ Have as much fun as possible.
- ➢ Be as creative as you like.
- ➢ Don't eat the rice.

How to make a Rice Box

- ➢ To make your Rice Box simply pour the rice into the plastic tote box.
- ➢ Add the funnels and cups to the rice. That's it!

Teaching Tips

Below are two different ways that the Rice Box can be used. The first option requires guided instruction.

The second option provides an activity children can do independently or with an adult. The second activity is great to keep in a mindfulness space and to use as an alternative to time out.

HOW TO USE THE RICE BOX

Meditation on the senses

> ➤ Have your child or children sit next to the Rice Box.
> ➤ Instruct your child(ren) to feel the rice with their hands. Allow them a few minutes to do this.
> ➤ Then, instruct your child(ren) to scoop the rice into the cups and pour it through the funnels.
> ➤ Encourage your child(ren) to listen to the sound of the rice as it falls through the funnels.
> ➤ Allow your child(ren) to continue exploring, feeling, and hearing with their senses as they work with the rice.

Free Exploration

> ➤ Have your child or children sit next to the Rice Box.
> ➤ Allow your child or children to play in the Rice Box with the funnels and cups.
> ➤ You can play with your child(ren) or allow them to play on their own.

Conclusion

The second activity is great to keep in a mindfulness space and to use as an alternative to time out. I recommend using this activity when your child is in the early stages of becoming upset. It is also a useful tool to employ before bed if your child has difficulty relaxing or falling asleep.

Creative Cat

There is a plethora of ways to make the Rice Box more dynamic. A few of them include dying the rice colors with food coloring, adding beans or other textured items, adding small toys, people, animals, etc. Be as creative as you would like. Allow your child's imagination to weigh in.

HOW TO MAKE A STRESS BALL

> ➤ Balloons: two balloons per stress ball.
> ➤ Flour and/or beans: 1/2 a cup of flour and or beans per stress ball.
> ➤ Funnel: 1 standard kitchen funnel.

Teaching Tips

Stress Balls can be made in a variety of textures. The recipe below contains instructions on how to make Stress Balls from flour. Kids enjoy having Stress Balls containing a variety of textures. The change in texture can help draw their attention. In order to do this, each child makes 3 Stress Balls. The first one is flour only, the second one is a combination of flour and small beans, and the third one is only beans. In order to make the different textured Stress Balls, change the ingredient in step 2.

8 Steps for Making a Stress Ball

STEP 1: First take a balloon and attach it to the smaller end of a funnel. Make sure the balloon is secure.

STEP 2: Pour about 1/4 of a cup of flour into the funnel.

STEP 3: Tap the sides of the funnel. This helps the flour flow into the funnel more easily.

STEP 4: Continue filling the balloon until it is 75% of the way full.

STEP 5: Tie the balloon.

STEP 6: Doubling the balloon–take another balloon and turn it inside out. Next, stuff the original balloon inside.

STEP 7: Tie the outer balloon.

STEP 8: Use the extra balloon material from above the knot and use it to cover the ball a third time. This gives the stress ball a clean look and adds and extra layer of protection.

Conclusion

Practice using the Stress Ball and feeling the varying textures between the different balls.

Creative Cat

The contents of the balloons can be changed to create a wide variety of textures. Some additional suggestions for filling are: kinetic sand, beach sand, seeds, and rice.

WALKING MEDITATION

Walking Meditation

This chapter provides instructions on how to teach Walking Meditation.

Tips for Teachers

You can do Walking Meditation inside or outside. You need enough space for the kids to be able to take approximately 10 steps. This activity can be performed in a circle, as a group, or individually in a line.

CIRCLE STYLE

Set-up

Have the children form a circle. If you are in a classroom, the perimeter of the classroom works great.

The Exercise

➢ Have each student stand approximately 1 foot part (if you don't have enough room, choose a smaller distance).

- Instruct the kids that once the group begins to move, they need to move at the same pace as the person in front of them. This means there should always be one foot between them and the person in front of them.

- Have the kids begin moving. It may be beneficial to either lead the group yourself or choose a leader that sets the pace.

- Periodically, have the group stop, face the center of the circle, and take a deep breath. Then, continue moving.

- To complete the activity, have the group again stop and face the center of the room. Have them take a moment to notice the faces of everyone else in the room.

LINE STYLE

Set-up

Have each child find a place where they can take 10 steps without crossing paths with anyone else.

The Exercise

- Instruct the kid(s) to mark a path wherein they can take 10 steps.

- Instruct the kids to slowly walk the marked path back and forth in silence.

- While they are walking, give them instructions on the different senses and sensations to focus on.
- Begin with having them feel their feet in each part of the moment.
- Then have them focus on things they hear as they are walking.
- Next, have them focus on things they smell as they are walking.
- Next, have them focus on things they see while they are walking.
- Lastly, instruct them to breath air in through their mouth and notice if they taste anything in the air.
- End the activity by having all participants return to their initial position and reflect on the experience.

The Exercise

This is a great exercise to use with kids who have a difficult time sitting still. Once the children are familiar with the concept of Walking Mediation, you can use it with them anywhere.

REFERENCES

Brown, P. L. (2007, June 16). In the classroom, and new focus on quieting the mind. *The New York Times* [New York]. Retrieved from http:/www.nytimes.com

Burke, C. A. (2010). Mindfulness-Based approaches with children and adolescents: A preliminary review of current research in an emergent field. *Journal of Child and Family Studies*. doi:10.1007/s10826-009-9282-x

Garbarino, J., & DeLara, E. (2002). *And words can hurt forever: How to protect adolescents from bullying, harassment, and emotional violence.* New York: Free Press.

Hochman, D. (2013, November 13). Mindfulness: Getting Its Share of Attention - The New York Times. Retrieved from http://www.nytimes.com/2013/11/03/fashion/mindfulnessand-meditation-are-capturing-attention.html

Kabat-Zinn, J. (2003). Mindfulness-Based Interventions in Context: Past, Present, and Future. *Clinical Psychology-science and Practice.* doi:10.1093/clipsy/bpg016

Lantieri, L. (2008). Building inner resilience. *Reclaiming Children and Youth, 17(2),* 43-46.

Lantieri, L., Kyse, E. N., Harnett, S., & Malkmus, C. (2011). Building inner resilience in teachers and students. In G. M. Reevy & E. Frydenberg(Eds.), *Personality, stress, and coping: Implications for education* (267-292). Charlotte, NC: Information Age Publishing, Inc.

Lantieri, L. (2014). *The inner resilience program*. Retrieved from: http://innerresilience.org

Mendelson, T., Greenberg, M. T., Dariotis, J. K., Gould, L. F., Rhoades, B. L., & Leaf, P. J. (2010). Feasibility and preliminary outcomes of a school-based mindfulness intervention for urban youth. Journal of *Abnormal Child Psychology*. doi:10.1007/ s10802-010-9418-x

Razza, R. A. (2013). Enhancing preschoolers' self-regulation via mindful yoga. Journal of *Child and Family Studies*.

Saltzman, A., & Goldin, P. (2008). Mindfulness-based stress reduction for school-age children. Acceptance and mindfulness interventions for children adolescents and families.

Schonert-Reichl, K. A., & Lawlor, M. S. (2010). The effects of a Mindfulness-Based Education program on pre and early adolescents' well-being and social and emotional competence. *Mindfulness*. doi:10.1007/s12671-010-0011-8

Simon, A., Harnett, S., Nagler, E. & Thomas, L. (2009). Research on the effect of the inner resilience program on teacher and student wellness and classroom climate: Final report. New York: Metis Associates.

UCLA Mindful Awareness Research Center | UCLA Mindful Awareness Research Center. (2015). Retrieved from http://marc.ucla.edu

Zoogman, S., Goldberg, S. B., & Hoyt, W. T. (2014). Mindfulness Interventions with youth: A meta-analysis.

ABOUT THE AUTHOR

and Yoga Teacher with a private practice in Longwood, Florida (Orlando Area). Kirsten holds a Master's degree from Syracuse University and a Bachelors Degree from the University of California Santa Cruz. Through Kirsten's *therapy practice, workshops, groups,* retreats, and *online courses,* she leads people to address the lack of connection in their lives. Kirsten is best known for inspiring others to revolutionize their lives through understanding and harnessing their holistic and powerful nature. For more information about Kirsten and additional resources visit: https://kirstenkeach.com.

Made in the USA
San Bernardino, CA
01 August 2017